erfect life an imp... an i

erfect life an imperfect life an i

an imperfect life

jodi hills

TRISTAN Publishing
Minneapolis

To my imperfect family,
to my imperfect friends,
I love you with all of my imperfect heart.

jodi hills

Copyright © 2008 Jodi Hills

TRISTAN Publishing Inc.
2355 Louisiana Avenue North
Golden Valley, MN 55427

ISBN 978-0-931674-91-4
Printed in China
First Printing

Please visit www.tristanpublishing.com

I wish for you an imperfect life -
and all the wonder that living can bring...
the wealth that comes from knowing loss,
the tears that find their way to laughter,
the joy that grows after the rain,
and the love, felt deepest,
by those who have been carved by pain.
I hope that you can value this imperfection,
hold on to it,
so it gives you such comfort
that you will dare embrace the beauty
of all the imperfect lives that surround you,
and then you will be perfectly free
to step to the beat of your own imperfect heart,
and you will have truly lived.

It's kind of exciting, the morningtime...
when you wake up and realize
not only who you are,
but all the possibilities of who you can be.

Sometimes she wondered if everyone had a map but her. Did they all actually know where they were going? Did they have the directions to the "happily ever after?" And if they did know, why did they never stop?
So what if she didn't have a map.
She had good strong legs, strong enough to chase the "happily ever after"…
and a strong enough heart to know that sometimes, stopping to enjoy the "happily right now" was pretty good too.

My feet,
with their need
for solid ground,
couldn't
convince
my heart
not to set sail.

"What if it doesn't happen?"
People are so quick, almost eager,
to prepare you for the worst.
If I give you nothing else,
I'll try to prepare you for the best,
and maybe, just maybe,
you'll believe it's ok to hope for it,
work for it, wait for it,
and embrace it when it comes...
I'll be the one saying to you, and myself,
"The best could happen....
and what if it does, what if it does!"

I've survived "no,"
cheered along with "yes"
and tiptoed through "maybe"-
all the while learning what I want
is not always what I need,
yet I must never be afraid to ask.

She wasn't where she had been.
She wasn't where she was going...
but she was on her way.
And on her way she enjoyed
food that wasn't fast, friendships that held,
hearts glowing, hearts breaking,
smiles that caught tears,
paths trudged and alleys skipped.
And on her way she no longer looked for the answers,
but held close the two things she knew for sure.
One, if a day carried strength in the morning,
peace in the evening,
and a little joy in between,
it was a good one...
and two, you can live completely
without complete understanding.
She was on her way.

Sometimes,
when you run,
people think you're running away.
And that may be partially right...
but sometimes
you're trying to get to somewhere...
get to a place that will fill your soul
with a love that says
they've been waiting just for you,
and a forgiveness
that doesn't care how you got there.

They say, "Be Yourself,"
like you know exactly what that is…
like you're a toaster or something…
like there's only that one way to pop out you.
Well maybe being me isn't just one thing.
Maybe just searching for me is being me
and not being them - being themselves…being toasters.
Maybe being me is more like a breakfast cereal variety pack.
Maybe that's what I'll be…today.
But tomorrow, who knows?...
maybe the blue plate special.

Sometimes she would catch herself,
not waiting for anything,
but just enjoying the moment...
and even though, in catching herself
she ended the moment,
she would smile,
knowing that another would come along,
and in a moment of happiness
is always a good place to catch yourself.

If you're craving words
like "you're beautiful" or
"I love you,"
don't go without,
tell them to yourself
and believe them.

She took comfort

in the pure randomness
that surrounded her,
accepting that no one escapes,
knowing that it could happen to anyone, at any time...
pain, happiness, confusion,

even love.

I climb.

I hope.

I reach.

I pray.

I curse.

I kick.

I laugh.

I rest.

I climb.

I hope.

These stairs, my life.

Someday, I imagine,
I will take down my heart fences and
simply say, "I love you,"
and I won't be safe,
but I will be saved.

With time, the things that make me care seem to change.
Tears and laughter often reverse their roles.
The world switches from big to small
depending on the uncertainties that surround us,
while comfort packs its bags and moves from place to place,
never leaving a forwarding address.
But through the impermanence of people and feelings,
you stay as slow, as warm and as forever
as children's summer laughter.
You remain a part of my heart's truth
the part that doesn't get crushed
beneath the weight of time passing,
the part I give thanks for, every day.

I can't take the chance that you don't know
how much it means to me,
you carrying my hopes like precious cargo,
and traveling with me to dreams come true...
so I will tell you again and again,
as if it were the first time,
"It is an honor,
it is a privilege,
it is a joy,
to share with you the path."

There are some souls on this earth that just seem to shine a little brighter. It's not because they've been left to burn in peace and quiet. I think it's because they've been stirred - and poked, and prodded.
The fire grows and glows because of the beautiful struggle they're in.
The flame gets a little hotter,
the heart a little stronger,
and the soul so very, very, bright.
You shine.

It was so windy that day,
I couldn't stand up straight.
It blew my hair this way and that way,
and sucked the tears right out of my eyes.

It was so windy that day.
I tried to tell you I loved you,
but you couldn't hear me.
Deaf to my cries, your ears heard a different calling.

It was so windy that day.
On hands and knees I crawled to your side.
I reached up to you, begged you to hang on.
I closed my eyes with visions of our hands joined,
like they were before the storm.
The wind shook my insides, leaving me hollow.
I opened my eyes and you were gone.
It was so windy that day.

What used to blow through me, now gives me wings

If she did worry, it never showed in her hands.

She held.

She gave.

She touched.

Not all of her dreams came true,
but she was never sorry she had them.

Dream it anyway.

It's been a while since I've been hit by a train,
so forgive me if I'm not sure what to do,
who to call,
or how to act.
I just can't believe I didn't hear the whistle,
or see the flashing lights
before I got knocked off the road...

I need to sit here for a bit and catch my breath.
I'm not sure of a lot right now,
but I do know I'm not going to stay with the wreckage,
or carry it with me...
I am going to catch my breath,
and walk on.

If I'm not happy in this time,
in this place,
I'm not paying attention.

When they asked her how she had survived,
she took a deep breath,
as if the answer was filling her,
"We breathe instinctively, don't we..." she said,
pausing, as faith, luck and gratitude turned a smile.
"I guess, after a while, I just let my heart follow."

She knew it was a big girl world...
and most of the time, she enjoyed being one...
She had paid her dues with every skinned knee
and lesson learned -
"Gotta be a big girl," they said -
and she was...
She could handle what was placed in front of her,
and what was taken away.
She could make the decisions and pay the rent.
But it was her heart that sometimes longed
for the lap of security, the gentle "there, there,"
the worry-free, sunny day in the backyard,
the ease with which that little girl gave love out,
and let love in...

She knew it was a big girl world,

but sometimes it felt really good,
when she allowed herself some of the simple pleasures
of just being small.

They laughed a little louder,
they cried a little softer,
they lived a little stronger,
because they stood together...
friends.

If I were a house,

I would be a big, yellow house,

with a yellow so inviting that if you were to walk by,

just being you, it would call to you,

"Come in, you and your heart sit down."

And if you did,

come into that big, yellow, inviting house,

you'd know you were home.

She woke each morning with a glow of hope,
not because a new dream had been born,
but knowing the one she carried in her heart would last.

People are so complicated,
so strange and different, with all their dreams and struggle
When you look closely at all of the disguises,
hopes and flaws -
the fast and slow music of confusion that surrounds them,
causing this ballet of untimely movement -
they're really quite beautiful, you know...

All the possibilities that lie within

send them fumbling towards grace
with just a turn of an imperfect lip,
or the touch of a worn hand.
It's what keeps me going -
knowing that somewhere inside of them - inside of me -
are all these strange, complicated,
different and beautiful possibilities.

The healing began when she realized
there wasn't a hole in her heart, but an opening.

Understanding that
heavy things can't fly,
she let go of what was weighing on her heart,
the things she could no more control than carry,
and she gave herself a chance,
a chance to reach into the unassuming blue,
to embrace the possibility of an open sky,
with an open heart.
She gave herself
a chance to soar.

Realizing how much this dream
could change her life,
her life already started to change.

Grace sat with me,

until I could walk in it again.

Again, I live this day
for the first time.
I feel the possibility of this brand new sky, again,
and I make promises to the world and myself
that I will make the most of this moment
again and again.
And I make the same mistakes for the first time -
and I cry old tears - and smile new hopes -
and I try and I laugh and I hurt,
and I pray for answers to the same old questions,
asked again and again -
when the answer is still and again - love.
I am blanketed by the night sky
and dream sweet and scared
and happy again - to wake to this day
for the first time -
to live in the possibility of this brand new sky,
and love, like I never thought I would, again.

Today I belong here...

tomorrow, if I don't, it doesn't mean
that I never did, or that I never will again.
My home travels with me.

I saw the truth about you -
the truth in how you could take life's punch,
the hurt in wondering why you had to,
the strength in your surviving smile.
I saw the truth about you, and it was BEAUTIFUL!
I questioned why all hadn't bothered to look.
Maybe they were afraid to view the extraordinary mess,
because there comes a responsibility with that -
once you acknowledge that you've seen someone,
you're involved, you're a part of it -
a part of all the imperfect truth.
I saw the truth about you -
the honesty in the struggle surpassed,
the truth in the tears, the laughter,
the pain, the love, and the glorious joy
that only comes from life's truest moments.
I saw the truth about you - and the truth is,
I give thanks for that, every day.

Just because someone's not waiting,
doesn't mean you have
nowhere to go.

Let someone in.

Let someone go.

After you've seen it all,
you won't remember the windows and doors,
but who passed through.

And so it begins,
looking to find that reason to believe
in something, in someone...
and no less important,
looking to be found.

erfect life an imperfect life an i

erfect life an imperfect life an i